$25.00

CHAMBER MUSIC

'JOISSANCE VOUS DONNERAY MON AMY'
Three ladies performing this famous French chanson
Painting by 'the Master of the Half Figures' c. 1530, Count Harrach's Collection, Vienna

A. HYATT KING

CHAMBER MUSIC

WITH 7 PLATES IN COLOUR
& 33 BLACK-AND-WHITE
ILLUSTRATIONS

GREENWOOD PRESS, PUBLISHERS
WESTPORT, CONNECTICUT

Library of Congress Cataloging in Publication Data

King, Alexander Hyatt.
    Chamber music.

    Reprint of the ed. published by M. Parrish, London;
Chanticleer Press, New York, which was issued as v. 3
of The World of music.
    Bibliography: p.
    1. Chamber music—History and criticism.
I. Series: The World of music (London) ; 3.
ML1100.K5 1979   785.7   78-60140
ISBN 0-313-20546-9

Reprinted with the permission of Chanticleer Press, Incorporated

Reprinted in 1979 by Greenwood Press, Inc.,
51 Riverside Avenue, Westport, CT 06880

Printed in the United States of America

10 9 8 7 6 5 4 3 2 1

CONTENTS

PLATES IN COLOUR

The colour plates have been reproduced in black and white in the reprint edition.

ILLUSTRATIONS IN BLACK & WHITE

The Editors wish to thank Mr. Paul Hirsch who kindly put his library at their disposal

To M.B.K.

We are indebted to the following for permission to reproduce the pictures in this book : Colour : page 37, the Trustees of the National Gallery ; page 38, the Walker Art Gallery, Liverpool ; page 55, the Leicester Galleries ; page 56, Mr. Joseph Lüscher. Black-and-White on the following pages : 9, the Curators of the Bodleian Library ; 13, 14, 23, 25, 51, the Trustees of the British Museum ; 16, 17, Messrs. D. Anderson, Rome ; 33, Les Archives Photographiques, Paris ; 43, Photographische Gesellschaft, Berlin ; 53, Museum der Stadt Wien; 63, the Committee of Manchester Corporation Galleries; 65, the Librarian of the Bournemouth Public Library; 67, Mrs. Ethel Macmillan ; 69, Miss Stella Schmolle

I

'THE MUSIC OF FRIENDS'

N the early history of music there are various types of composition of whose origin and evolution we still know comparatively little. The work of scholars of many nations in the last sixty or seventy years has shed some light on the growth of vocal music, but much remains to be discovered and clarified concerning instrumental music. This is quite reasonable, if we remember that singing is a more natural and a much older form of self-expression than playing; in fact, up to about 1600 far more music had been written for voices than for instruments. It was about the middle of the sixteenth century that "chamber music" began to evolve from an intricate mass of styles, names and forms.

We know precisely the years when opera and oratorio came into being, but no such date can be given for "chamber music", though the partial derivation of the term does at least suggest its probable place of origin. In the 1580's in Italy a favourite type of composition was the *sonata da camera*, a phrase that has two important connotations: it was music that was "sounded" (*sonata*), as distinct from music that was sung (*cantata*), and it was intended for performance in the chamber or *camera* of a prince's court, and therefore written on fundamentally different principles from the *musica da chiesa* (church music) or from operatic music.

Quite early in its history we find in chamber music one characteristic which differentiated it from all other instrumental forms: *the playing of the individual parts by a single instrument*. This characteristic has remained constant, however much the scope and meaning of the term has varied from age to age. Many of the types of chamber music, too, are very flexible in

MUSICIANS OF THE 13TH CENTURY
MS. written for Alfonso X. Escorial

their implication. Thus, though the smallest number of parts in a chamber work is two, such a piece is mostly called a sonata (though this applies equally to a solo instrument) and much less often a "duo". In this, one part is usually for piano, and the other may be written for anything from a flute to a double-bass. A "trio" commonly implies a piano with two stringed or two wind instruments, or with one stringed and one wind, but may also be three stringed or three wind unsupported by the keyboard. The quartet and quintet are most often composed for stringed instruments, but can admit as much variety as the trio. With sextets, septets and octets, wind instruments tend to predominate, at any rate in the eighteenth century, though unmixed strings became popular in the nineteenth. Obviously the possible variety of combinations increases with the number of the parts. Although in recent times a chamber work rarely exceeds ten parts, and the line of demarcation between this and one for small orchestra has become blurred, one profound truth stands out from difficulties of definition, obscurity of origin and changes of fashion—real chamber music has always been "the music of friends". As such, it is one of the most uplifting, cultured and pleasurable pursuits that European civilisation has produced.

The three countries where conditions of life were most favourable to such a fragile growth were Italy, England and Spain. (It is a curious and notable fact that Germany and Austria, the two lands most closely associated with the classical period of chamber music—roughly from 1730 to 1830—made practically no original contribution to its early development.) In these three parts of Europe the music that was played in the royal courts, in the castles of the nobility and in the houses of the wealthier gentry went through nearly parallel stages of growth. Very few extant instrumental compositions date from before 1500; but pictures, engravings, illuminated manuscripts and official documents portray the types of instruments, and reveal their names and something of how they were played. Precisely what the music was and how it developed remains rather a mystery until the second half of the sixteenth century, when instrumental works began to be printed in quantities comparable to the mass of vocal music that the presses poured out from 1530 onwards.

In Italy at this time the oldest and most popular musical form was the madrigal, a secular composition for unaccompanied voices, ranging from two to five or six parts. Gradually the voices were found to be interchangeable with instruments whose compass nearly corresponded with that of the original singers. Thus Giovanni Bassano (*flor. c.* 1600) published at Venice in 1585 *Fantasie a tre voci, per cantar et sonar con ogni sorte d'Istrumenti* (Fantasias for three voices, to be sung and played on all sorts of instruments) and in the same year a collection entitled *Ricercarte, Passagi e Cadentie,* written in an elaborately ornamented and repetitive style which undoubtedly originated as an accompaniment to dances with

MUSICIANS OF THE 13TH CENTURY
MS. written for Alfonso X.   Escorial

regularly repeating figures. Among a large number of excellent musicians active at this time three specially deserve mention. Floriano Canali (1575-1603), though mainly a vocal composer, left a notable collection of instrumental *canzoni* in eight parts. Salomone Rossi (*flor.* 1587-1628), who was of Jewish origin and a colleague of Monteverdi at Mantua, was one of the first to appreciate the possibilities of the new style, and wrote little three-part "sonatas" of distinctly instrumental character. Biagio Marini (*c.* 1597-1665) won great distinction as a solo violinist, and travelled widely, especially in Germany, where he popularised his development of the three-part sonatas that were to have such a long and important vogue in European music.

Meanwhile, a similar development had been taking place in England. It seems reasonably certain that here instrumental music had attained the stature of an art-form earlier than in any other country. Concerning its growth we know very little, but about 1495 Hugh Aston wrote a "hornpipe" for the virginals in a masterly style which presumes a considerable ancestry. Instrumental music flourished in the courts of Henry VII and Henry VIII (himself a composer of pieces for viols), and at the death of the latter in 1547 an inventory made by order of Edward VI lists hundreds of instruments, including lutes, viols, virginals, organs, shawms, recorders, flutes, cornets, guitars and horns. Such remarkable numbers and varieties suggest a great deal of music-making, and this is confirmed by rather vague references in official records. But little survives of what was then played, nor do we know which of the instruments were used together for chamber purposes or precisely when this synthesis took place. One group, however, the viols, was so employed, and the "chest of viols", as it was called, became practically synonymous with chamber music for the best part of a century, from about 1550.

All through the sixteenth century Italian influences on the tastes and manners of the upper classes in England had been very strong, and in 1588 the invasion of the Italian madrigal won a signal victory with the publication of Nicholas Yonge's *Musica Transalpina*. This was a collection of fifty-seven madrigals by famous Italian composers, which despite the crudeness of some of the English versions was so successful that it was followed by a second book. From 1590 onwards we find on many title-pages of madrigals composed by English musicians such words as "apt for viols and voyces", the equivalent of Bassano's "per cantar et sonar". English musicians were quick to appreciate the possibilities of composing chamber works in a style less imitative of vocal music, and the "fancy" (corresponding to the Italian "fantasia") came into being. Its manner was "polyphonic", that is, consisting of several freely-moving and apparently independent parts that were, however, related harmonically. The style and aesthetic purpose of the fancy were fairly uniform: it was a free exercise of the musical imagination based on the use of "imitation", that is, the repetition of a phrase by another voice or part than that which first states it. A simple piece of melody was thus developed with brilliant technical ingenuity. Often a second theme was introduced when every drop of expression had been squeezed out of the first. In this guise English chamber music was launched upon its brief but glorious career. The exquisitely printed title-pages of the published works (far fewer than those still in manuscript) faithfully set forth the nature and scope of this lovely music, in language as "fanciful" as its style.

In 1599 appeared Anthony Holborne's *Pavans, Galliards, Almains and other short Aeirs, both grave and light, in five parts for viols, violins and other musical*

CHAMBER MUSIC IN VENICE, C. 1500
Two lutes and a rebec
Sketch by Vittore Carpaccio

instruments; in 1604, Dowland's *Lachrimæ, or Seaven Teares figured in Seaven Passionate Pavans, with divers other Pavans, Galiards and Alemands, set forth for the lutes, viols or violons in five parts*; in 1630 an important work by Martin Peerson, *Mottects or Grave Chamber Musique. Containing songs of five parts of several sorts, some ful, and some verse and chorus. But all fit for voyces and Vials, with an organ part.* Here we have the first use of the phrase "chamber music" in English: Peerson's work was not purely instrumental, but neither were many of the other chamber works both before and during this time, and the tradition of vocal chamber music has lasted right down to the twentieth century. Though Italian in its original inspiration, the work of these and many other composers soon became as thoroughly English in feeling and idiom as the madrigals of Wilbye and Weelkes.

Nor was the greatness of their art confined to England: it is one of the least known but most interesting facts in musical history that English composers exercised a widespread influence in Germany from the beginning of the seventeenth century right down to the 1660's. John Dowland, Thomas Simpson, Walter Rowe and William Brade were among those who

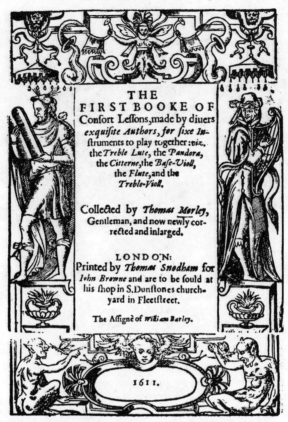

THE
FIRST BOOKE OF
Confort Leſſons, made by diuers
exquiſite Authors, for ſixe In-
ſtruments to play together: *viz.*
the *Treble Lute,* the *Pandora,*
the *Citterne,* the *Baſe-Violl,*
the *Flute,* and the
Treble-Violl.

Collected by *Thomas Morley,*
Gentleman, and now newly cor-
rected and inlarged.

LONDON:
Printed by *Thomas Snodham* for
Iohn Browne and are to be ſould at
his ſhop in S. Dunſtones church-
yard in Fleetſtreet.

The Aſſigne of *William Barley.*

1611.

COLLECTION OF MUSIC FOR 'BROKEN CONSORT'
Made by Thomas Morley, 1611

held posts in the German courts and trading cities, and either taught the instruments of chamber music, or published collections of it with German imprints. Some of these collections—such as Thomas Simpson's *Taffel Consort*, published at Hamburg in 1621—contain works by English composers which are virtually unknown in their native land. And as the century wore on, German musicians came to England for instruction, especially on the favourite viola da gamba—the "viol de gamboys" of *Twelfth Night.* English music also found its way into the repertoire of the *Collegia Musica,* the chamber-music societies which were then flourishing in many parts of

A VIOL-PLAYER
From Christopher Simpson's 'Division Violist', 1659

Germany despite the Thirty Years War. The German writers who two centuries later dubbed England "Land ohne Musik" found it convenient to forget (if indeed they ever knew) that once their country was England's musical debtor.

In Spain, the practice of chamber music was of great antiquity, greater perhaps than in any other country. In the cathedral at Pamplona there exists a finely carved ivory box made in Cordoba in 1005, and showing an ensemble of a lute, a double pipe and a kind of viol. Miniatures in MSS. preserved in the Escorial and other libraries, dating from the thirteenth

STILL LIFE OF MUSICAL INSTRUMENTS AND MUSIC
The parts for 'Madrigals for Six Voices' by Peter Philips on the music stand
Detail from 'Hearing' by Jan Brueghel, c. 1620. Prado, Madrid

century, continue the tale: they show us various combinations, including viol and tambourine, lute and tambourine, guitar and harp. Three hundred years later a long passage in the second book of a novel called *Diana* by Montemayor, written about 1560, gives a vivid picture of the playing of chamber music, and as this author had studied music in his youth, the details may be taken as quite trustworthy. A long episode in the second book includes a performance—given in the street, in the manner of the eighteenth-century serenade, but with true chamber characteristics—that opens with a piece for four wooden cornets and a sackbut. Next comes a long Spanish ballad sung to their accompaniment, followed by a duet for harp and oboe. After a song sung to the harp, the instrumentalists play a long piece for four viols and virginals, and a four-part madrigal leads to the grand finale in which took part "several different kinds of instruments and very excellent voices concerted with them".

A MUSIC PARTY
From the background of 'Hearing'
Painting by Jan Brueghel, c. 1620. Prado, Madrid

In France, chamber music was less assiduously cultivated at this time, but a few very gifted musicians, such as Claude Gervaise (*flor. c.* 1550) and Eustache du Caurroy (1549-1609) have left suites for viols ranging from three to six parts. It would seem that the origins of instrumental chamber music of this sort lie more in the evolution of dance forms than in the adaptation of vocal polyphony. But these smaller forms never took root in France, where musical taste was moulded by the artistic dictatorship of Louis XIV. He did establish a *Maître de la musique de la chambre du Roy*, but lent more favour to the spectacular ballet and opera, which could reflect and enhance his own glory. These, however, ran contrary to the spirit of private music-making which is the life-blood of true chamber music.

At this time music continued to flourish in the Netherlands despite the Spanish oppression. Though the tradition was mainly vocal, continuing that of the fifteenth and sixteenth centuries, there is reason to suppose that instrumental music was by no means neglected. The Prado at Madrid contains a picture by Jan Brueghel, entitled *El Oído* (Hearing), one of a series of five illustrating the senses. It shows all kinds of instruments scattered about the floor of a large room, and in another a group of seven people performing music from oblong part-books. Their disposition—three singers, and players on flute, oboe, bass-viol and lute—strongly suggests that the madrigal was being rendered partly as chamber music. On other music-stands are open part-books, in which can be read the name of Peter Philips, an English composer who lived all his life in the Netherlands. His music was published there between 1612 and 1630.

Up to the middle of the seventeenth century, the medium most favoured for the execution of chamber music was the "consort" of viols. This was either a "whole consort", consisting solely of viols, ranging from treble to bass, or a "broken consort" which included other instruments, both string and wind. In the extant printed music of this period, the latter is comparatively uncommon; we find it, for example, in 1611 in *The First Booke of Consort Lessons, made by divers exquisite authors, for sixe instruments to play together; viz. the treble lute, the pandora, the citterns, the base-violl, the flute and the treble-violl. Collected by Thomas Morley.* But the whole consort of viols held the stage for nearly a century, and as they differ in many respects from the violins, which coexisted with them and gradually took their place, they deserve to be described in some detail. Apart from differences in shape and acoustic design, a viol has five or six strings to the violin's four; being thinner and quite loosely stretched, the strings give a tone less brilliant, but purer and more easily produced; a flatter bridge allows easy playing of chords; all viols, of whatever size, are held downwards in playing, with the hand over the bow, and the hairs of the bow (which curves outwards, another aid to chord playing) can be loosened or tightened by the pressure of the fingers; the finger-board has movable gut frets to aid accurate intonation and clear tone. There is no doubt that these subtleties were related to the style and technical demands of the fancy. For, in general, the technique of the viol family is less exacting than that of the violin, and so was well suited to enable skilled amateurs to cope with the fluent and intricate contrapuntal style in which the music was mostly written. The usual number in a "chest" of viols was six—two treble, two tenor and two bass. The veiled richness of their contrasting registers and the intimate and delicate clarity of tone make an unforgettable experience for anyone who in recent years has been fortunate enough to hear the Dolmetsch family perform fancies by the masters of this great age of chamber music.

A Minstrel accompanied by Viella and Flute
Illumination representing the poet known as 'Kanzler'
From the Manesse Codex of Minnesingers, written in Zurich c. 1340

DUET FOR VIOLIN AND LUTE
Painting by Pieter de Hooch, 1667
By gracious permission of H.M. The King

II

THE RISE OF THE VIOLINS

ROADLY speaking, the viol was the dominant chamber instrument of the Renaissance; from the Baroque to our own age, the sovereignty of the violin has never been seriously challenged. Both types had evolved to their technical perfection by about 1550, but not until nearly a century later did the louder and more brilliant violin family begin to come into general use. Once it was established, the composing of chamber music as we understand the term to-day proceeded at a remarkable rate all over Europe, although in widely varying styles. The rise of the world-famous Cremonese violin-makers—the Amatis, Stradivari, and Ruggieri—spurred on the great Italian violinists to attain heights of astonishing virtuosity. A host of notable executants, many of whom were also fine composers, arose to continue the work of Marini, who, as we have seen, was one of the creators of the trio-sonata and made it popular through his travels in Germany. Trio-sonatas were composed in large numbers by such men as Legrenzi (1626-90), Vitali (c. 1640-92), Corelli (1653-1713), Tartini (1692-1770) and Locatelli (1693-1764), and were usually for two violins or flutes and "figured bass".

Since the "figured bass"—otherwise called the "basso continuo" or "thorough-bass"—was the corner-stone of all types of chamber music until well into the eighteenth century and to some extent governed its form, it requires some explanation. It was a kind of musical shorthand in which, under or above the single notes of the bass part, there were printed figures indicating, according to an accepted convention, the harmony desired by the composer. From these figures the player could construct the accompaniment, with considerable scope for invention and artistic elaboration in

the spacing and inverting of the chords. This system originated in the needs of church organists of the sixteenth century who often had to substitute for the choir or missing parts, and to this end arranged the bass parts of vocal compositions by marking with figures the harmonic successions which they had to fill out. Soon this usage spread to other types of music, with various instruments for the bass: at first, principally the lute and

ARCANGELO CORELLI
By J. Folkema
Engraving, c. 1715

violone (the largest of the viols, not admitted to the "consort" but originally much used for playing florid bass parts in Purcell, Bach and Handel), and later the harpsichord and violoncello, sometimes used in conjunction. This figured bass tended to absorb what had been the middle parts of the fancy, thus contrasting with the upper parts, which were now set free to develop into concerted music.

In chamber works particularly, this tendency was fostered by the brilliance of the violins, which became, as it were, vivid characters playing their part in the miniature dramas which, in truth, these trio-sonatas are. In the hands of its two greatest exponents in Italy, namely Legrenzi and Corelli, the trio-sonata attains full stature, having won complete independence from the vocal origins of the fancy, and bears comparison with the best chamber music of any era. The four short movements, derived originally from the

'FANTAZIA UPON ONE NOTE'
By Henry Purcell, c. 1659-95
First lines of autographed score

dance forms of the suite, become purely instrumental abstractions, covering a wide range of style, feeling and *tempi*. Simple song-like movements alternate with brilliant displays of part-writing.

Though this product of the Italian masters quickly spread all over musical Europe, in each country the style of the trios varied according to local tastes and traditions. In Germany many composers substituted for the second violin a viola da gamba whose rich, dark tone-colouring provided a contrast. Among the great German musicians who wrote trios were Pachelbel (1653-1706) and Buxtehude (1637-1707), both principally noted as organists. Towards the end of the century there appeared new chamber combinations based on the trio form. Of outstanding interest is the *Hortus Musicus* composed in 1704 by J. A. Reincken, a famous Hamburg organist whom the youthful Bach went far to hear. It was for two violins, viola da gamba and figured bass, and consists of thirty pieces, numbered consecutively, and forming six suites of spirited and delightful music. Bach himself left a considerable amount of fine chamber music, including one pure trio-sonata and three sets of sonatas for violin, flute and gamba respectively, all with keyboard accompaniment. Part of his *Musikalisches Opfer* (1747) consists of an exquisite movement for violin, flute and bass. Handel too excelled in the more intimate forms, and made a special contribution with the fifteen sonatas for two oboes and bass which enshrine some of his noblest inspirations.

In England, with changing social conditions, the art of the madrigal was moribund by 1635, and although the practice and composition of instrumental fancies lingered on for some time, their elaborate part-writing could not long withstand the disintegrating influence of solo violin-playing that spread from the Continent after the Restoration. William Lawes, a highly gifted musician killed at the siege of Chester in 1645, composed fancies for viols in three, four, five and six parts; in 1638 Michael East issued the seventh set of his three-part fancies: and in 1656 Matthew Locke published his *Little Consort* containing forty "Pavans, Ayres, Corants and Sarabands for Viols or Violins" in three parts. This last title, mentioning the alternative violins, is perhaps significant of the change in taste that was coming in. From the following account of chamber music in Oxford, written by the historian of that University, Anthony Wood (1632-95), it seems that in academic circles the viols continued to be preferred:

> The Gentlemen in privat meetings which I frequented played three, four and five part with viols, a treble viol, tenor viol, tenor, counter-tenor and bass, with an organ, virginal or harpsicon joyned with them; and they esteemed a violin to be an instrument only belonging to a common fidler, and could not endure that it should come among them for fear of making their meetings to be vain and fidling.

But the violin appears to have been publicly established by about 1660 when John Jenkins (1592-1678) is believed to have issued his own *Twelve Sonatas for Two Violins and a Base with a Thorough Base for the Organ or Theorbo.* Though this was probably the first English publication of violin chamber music, it had been composed some years earlier, among others by Benjamin Rogers who in 1653 presented some airs in four parts for violins and organ to the Archduke of Austria and a similar piece to Queen Christina of Sweden. Rogers's popularity serves to illustrate the continued influence of English chamber music in German lands, as does also the work of William Young

SINGERS ACCOMPANIED BY HARPSICHORD AND VIOLIN
Sketch by Thomas Gainsborough, 1727–88

(d. 1672), a domestic musician at the court of Innsbruck, who in 1653 published 21 sonatas for three violins, viola and bass.

At this period many passages in the diaries of Evelyn and Pepys attest the enthusiasm of London society for chamber playing, which took place in clubs such as those run by John Banister and Thomas Britton, as well as in private houses. There was also much music-making, on a rather lower social plane, in inns and taverns all over the country where small groups of professional musicians used to entertain and sometimes annoy travellers by playing both during supper and outside bedroom doors to rouse them in the morning!

By far the greatest Stuart composer of chamber music, and indeed of any other kind of music, was Henry Purcell (1659–95). Those of his works which concern us here fall into two distinct classes, one reflecting his youthful devotion to old traditions, the other his study of the new Italian style. The fantasias for strings, that is viols, are in three, four and five parts, and date from about 1680; the two sets of sonatas in three and four parts (for two violins, bass and continuo) were published respectively in 1683 and 1697. The fantasias are the swan-song of the golden age of English chamber music: they combine all the resources of contrapuntal imitation with a highly personal idiom and an almost unprecedented intensity of expression. One of the most masterly is the famous Fantasia on One Note in five parts, the fourth part consisting of middle C, repeated and held in every bar, round which the other instruments embroider a polyphonic pattern in a texture of ever-increasing complexity. Throughout, the instruments converse with the gracious serenity that is one of the hallmarks of true chamber music. Less intricate but no less delightful is the discourse of the sonatas, in his preface to the first edition of which Purcell wrote that he had "faithfully endeavour'd a just imitation of the most fam'd Italian masters". Nevertheless the idiom is just as personal as that of the fantasias, and the structure more varied than that of the trio-sonatas of Legrenzi and Corelli.

But Purcell had no true heirs, and for the next two centuries English chamber music was at its nadir. In the hands of competent but uninspired composers such as William Babell (*c.* 1690-1723), Charles Stanley (1713-86) and Joseph Gibbs (1699-1788) the trio-sonata showed surprising vitality. It even survived the domination of Handelian opera, and was still composed and published in great numbers well after Haydn's quartets had been imported into England. William Boyce, famous as the editor of *Cathedral Music*, published a charming set of trios in 1747, and a set by Pergolesi was imported as late as 1780.

DR. SYNTAX, TWO LADIES AND A PAGE
Vignette from the 'Third Tour', 1823 ed.
Coloured aquatint by Thomas Rowlandson

HARPSICHORD, VIOLIN AND 'CELLO
Engraving from the trio op. 80 by Joseph Haydn
Published by Artaria, 1798

III

'ALL FOR YOUR DELIGHT'

NOTED musical historian of the nineteenth century, W. S. Rock-stro, wrote in the first edition of Grove's *Dictionary* (1889) that "the rising fame of Haydn and Mozart placed between the School of Vienna and that of the Bachs a fathomless abyss which no amount of critical ingenuity will ever satisfactorily bridge over." It speaks volumes for the musical research of the last few generations that this abyss *has* been almost completely bridged over; we now know that this bridge consisted chiefly of the works of the composers who contributed to the perfecting of what is known as sonata form. And with this most fascinating period of musical evolution the growth of chamber music is intimately connected. When J. S. Bach died in 1750, an epoch died with him, and a general reaction set in against the somewhat florid baroque style. Experimenters all over Europe soon concerned themselves mainly with the smaller forms, especially those which were to evolve into the string quartet. The natural question "Who wrote the first quartet?" is not easy to answer definitely, and the answer partly depends on the meaning we attach to the term.

Allegri (1582-1652) composed what is undoubtedly very early violin music in four parts; about 1715 Alessandro Scarlatti (1659-1725) left a string

quartet expressly marked *senza cembalo*, in addition to over sixty beautiful
cantatas for solo singer accompanied by instruments, to which he accorded
the individuality proper to chamber music; Tartini (1692-1770), best known
to-day for his "Devil's Trill" Sonata, wrote a number of *quadri* quite free
from the figured bass. But in these and similar efforts we cannot always be
certain by how many instruments each part was meant to be played, and
furthermore the structure of the music was largely based on the trio-sonata
and its cognate forms. The classical quartet as we understand it did not
spring complete and radiant from the head of any musical Zeus. It is true
that one man, Joseph Haydn (1732-1809), breathed into its members the
divine spark of genius, but those members were shaped originally by many
now forgotten musicians, often working independently. The two principal
centres of really progressive activity were Mannheim and Vienna.

The former contained the court of the Elector Palatine, Duke Carl
Theodor (1724-99), one of the most lavish patrons of the arts and sciences
ever known. Many of the musicians in his establishment were ardent
devotees of chamber music, pre-eminent being the Stamitzes (Johann and
his sons Carl and Anton), F. X. Richter and Giuseppe Toeschi. In Vienna,
the brilliant centre of musical activity was the Imperial Court of the Haps-
burg Empire, closely linked with the great houses of the noblemen, many
of whom kept private musicians, as did also the powerful bishops in out-
lying towns such as Salzburg and Grosswardein (Oradea Mare). Composers
from many lands flocked into the capital, absorbed the latest notions, added
their own contribution, and then, as their profession became overcrowded,
were forced out again to seek employment far afield, in France, Russia,
Italy, Poland and England. A few went to Mannheim and continued the
good work there.

The most important results of this ferment of musical ideas between
1730 and 1750 can be briefly summed up thus: the figured bass, obsolescent
for some time, received its final quietus probably from the influence of
open-air playing (the harpsichord hardly being a mobile instrument), and
so allowed the equalisation of the parts to take shape; the general style of
music became less contrapuntal, drawing fresh inspiration from a more
flexible melodic line based on the rhythms of popular *divertimenti* and *cassations*; one of these rhythms, that of the minuet, crystallised into an artistic
and beautifully balanced piece which was added to the traditional three
movements of the old trio-sonata to make up the four of the symphony
and also of the quartet. Their first movements were now cast in the
"sonata form" which influenced the layout of the whole. Whereas

A CONCERT
From J. B. Basedow's 'Elementarwerk', 1774
Engraving by Daniel Chodowiecki

the trio-sonatas and fancies usually had one theme in each section, the quartet was now given two themes, or groups of themes, for discussion. Of these the second contrasted with the first in mood, line and key, which last was generally in the dominant—i.e. if the first theme was in C major, the second was in G major. The "working-out" of the movement depended for its success on the effective interplay and development of these two themes and their derivatives, in a scheme that postulated a restatement of the original material before a short coda, hinting at new possibilities, rounded off the whole.

We cannot, of course, expect to find these points of re-alignment con-centrated and fully exploited in the work of any one of the early Viennese composers. Chamber music at this time was in a state of flux, uncertain in design and purpose. Even in the music of such serious and worthy men as Christoph Wagenseil (1715-77), Georg Monn (1717-50) and Franz Asplmayr (c. 1728-86), there is much that is heterogeneous and spasmodic. They had cast off the sheet anchor of the baroque spirit, which was in no doubt that its artistic and spiritual mission was to exalt and convert, but were not quite reconciled to the unashamed avowal of the Rococo that its aim was "all for your delight". Some countries, of course, accepted this principle more readily than others: the attitude of French composers is perfectly summed up in the title of Gabriel Guillemain's *Six Sonates en Quatuors, ou Conversations Galantes et Amusantes entre une Flûtte Traversière, un Violon, une Basse de Viole et la Basse Continue* (1743), but the South Germans as a whole took a more serious view of musical art. Though Haydn's early efforts were just as tentative as those of his older contemporaries, he excelled them in the inventiveness with which he gradually brought out the individuality of all four instruments.

It seems probable that he stumbled on the quartet almost by accident. After he was dismissed from St. Stephen's Choir School in Vienna, he was cast on the world at the age of sixteen, and his self-education in music proceeded laboriously. But his early compositions, stamped with a vigorous personality, soon attracted attention in musical circles and among the nobility. In 1755, he was invited by Carl von Fürnberg to his country house at Weinzierl for a long stay during which were composed the eighteen works comprising op. 1, 2 and 3 of his Quartets. Of these the earliest were not called quartets at all, but passed under the popular names of *cassations*, *divertimenti*, or *notturni*, and are in fact little different from small-scale string symphonies of which the quartet is a refinement. One or two actually have optional horn parts, and most of the first two sets are in the five movements characteristic of true *divertimenti*. From 1759 to 1761 Haydn enjoyed his first regular employment as music director to Count Morzin, and when that nobleman disbanded his orchestra, Haydn's services were promptly engaged by Prince Paul Anton Esterházy, after whose death in 1762 they were retained by his brother Prince Nicolaus until 1790. It was during this period that Haydn composed most of his chamber music: his progress forms one of the most fascinating and important chapters in the history of music. Here we cannot do more than skim a few of its pages.

It was the fashion in the eighteenth century to compose and publish string quartets in sets of six, a good round number that gave scope for contrast and variety. The 36 quartets forming the sets famous the world over as Haydn's op. 1, 2, 3, 9, 17 and 20 are the perfect mirror of his technical and spiritual progress during the eighteen vital years 1755 to 1772. After beginning with bustling little pieces, naïve, "earthy" minuets and simple, lyrical melodies (such as that from op. 3, no. 5, popularly called Haydn's

'RULES AND ADVICE FOR THE PLAYING OF ALL THE BEST MUSICAL INSTRUMENTS'
Treatise in Spanish by Pablo Minguet y Yrol, 1752
Engraved frontispiece

"Serenade"), he gradually freed himself from the domination of the first violin. By learning to treat all four instruments on practically equal terms, he made the quartet a perfectly balanced, highly personal medium for the expression of his deepest feelings, as in the tragic and passionate works in C minor, op. 17, no. 4, and op. 20, no. 5. And what an exciting adventure it must have been for the chamber players at Esterház to rehearse the astonishing fugues that form the finales to op. 20, nos. 2, 5 and 6! Indeed, with op. 20 the first stage in the new art of chamber music came to an end.

Here we may take advantage of the ten-year pause in the composition of quartets to mention some of the other types of chamber music Haydn had written up to 1770, and was indeed to go on writing for more than twenty years. Twenty-one sonatas for two violins and bass are all early works, showing his attachment to the old trio-sonata, from which also evolved the trio for violin, 'cello and piano. Of these, between 1766 and 1798, he composed thirty: they contain some of his most original and spacious ideas, but are in fact sonatas for piano with string accompaniment; only in very few do the strings have a really important part. Among the best are the earliest of all in G minor (*c.* 1765), the famous one in G major containing the well-known Gipsy Rondo (*c.* 1795), the F sharp minor (*c.* 1790) a work of passionate melancholy alternating with lyrical sweetness, and a superb trio in E flat minor of 1798 which has much of the dynamic breadth of early Beethoven. Half-a-dozen duets for violin and viola, one for violin and 'cello, sonatas for violin and piano, a sonata for flute, harp and bass, a fine trio for horn, violin and 'cello, all bear witness to Haydn's ceaseless experimenting with forms both new and old. The famous (but doubtful) "Echo" Sextet of 1767 is pure chamber music of the Rococo: two trios, each of two violins and bass, were directed to play in adjacent rooms, invisible to each other but visible and audible to the select audience.

Excepting the quartets, the largest and in many ways the most interesting group consists of the 125 trios for baryton, viola and bass, composed over nearly twenty years for the private pleasure of Prince Nicolaus, who was a fine performer on the baryton. This was a late and rather cumbrous survivor of the viol family with six or seven strings, and a number of "sympathetic" strings under the bridge that were meant to be plucked by the player's thumb. Into these trios Haydn poured a wealth of delightful music, grave and gay, and found in them a safe field for many audacious experiments in form and texture of which the results were incorporated into his progressive mastery over the problems of the string quartet.

In 1781 Haydn completed op. 33, six quartets known as the "Russian". In these he announced to the world his great discovery, which turned on the principle of elaborating and expanding the chief melodies of the first move-ment in the "working-out" section that follows the opening statement. This principle was no less important for the growth of symphonies, concertos and piano sonatas than for chamber music, as its discoverer and his con-temporaries were quick to realise. He himself described the "Russian" quartets as being composed in a "new and special way", which really amounted to the concentration of the main interest of the first movement (for in the quartets usually only this is in sonata form) in the development section following the statement of the two groups of themes. This redistri-bution of interest actually affected the quality of Haydn's melodies, which became pregnant with suggestive power and endowed with hidden springs of energy to be kept in reserve for the development. Yet there was nothing

MOZART, AGED ELEVEN, PLAYING THE HARPSICHORD AT A TEA PARTY
In the salon of Prince Contí in Paris, 1766
Painting by Michel Barthélemy Ollivier, Louvre, Paris

ponderous in his application of this principle: the marvel of op. 33 is its blending of lightness and clarity with subtlety of form and complete individuality of each part.

Inspired by these works Mozart, twenty-four years Haydn's junior, composed and dedicated to him six quartets, from which Haydn in his turn learnt much. Indeed, Mozart's lyrical and essentially operatic genius was the only external influence on Haydn's music of the next ten years, especially his chamber works, which became ever more subtle and mellow. Even the four little trios for two flutes and 'cello, composed in 1794, in London, where the flute was the darling of musical society, are perfect of their kind.

Between 1784 and 1803 Haydn wrote 39 more quartets, each one a balanced masterpiece, each different from the last in the way in which the possibilities of the development section were exploited and refined. Haydn knew, better than any other composer, the secret of giving to a whole quartet that mysterious unity which seems to reflect in each movement a different aspect of one sharply-drawn character, forceful yet infinitely lovable and human. And this, combined with inexhaustible variety of mood, intimacy and warmth of expression, and an unfailingly logical progression towards the joyful consummation of each finale, makes the quartets of Haydn's maturity unique in the history of chamber music.

At the age of 14, Mozart began his career as an artist in chamber forms with a modest little quartet inspired mainly by similar works of Sammartini (1701-75), the incarnation of Italian lyrical sweetness. After three more uneventful quartets, disguised, like Haydn's early efforts, as *divertimenti*, Mozart composed in 1772 and 1773 two sets of six that are strongly coloured by his growing admiration for Haydn's music, and pay him the sincere tribute of imitating the fugal finales of his op. 20. There is no doubt that the more robust style of the older man's chamber music was a potent factor in helping Mozart to strengthen his own courtly and sometimes over-refined style. He triumphantly reached maturity in the six quartets which he composed in 1783 and 1784, and published with an affectionate dedication to Haydn in the next year. These six quartets, "the fruit of long and arduous toil" as he describes them in his dedication, are thoroughly German in tone, but also fraught with his own poetical tenderness and sensuous gaiety. Formally they do not represent an advance on Haydn's quartets: Mozart thankfully took over the principle of thematic expansion in the development section, and contented himself with refining and experimenting within this proven scheme. Some of his finales are particularly daring, such as the one to the Quartet in G, which consists of an alternation of an airy fugal structure with passages of lilting homophony. His minuets have a soaring grace almost unknown to the creations of Haydn's more boisterous fancy, but in some of his slow movements, notably the Tristanesque "brown study" of the Quartet in E flat, he is plainly modelling his thought on some of his friend's finest andantes.

This musical intercourse of Haydn and Mozart makes an absorbing study, rooted as it was in the friendliness of chamber music. Michael Kelly, the Irish singer who was resident in Vienna at this time, mentions in his

LEOPOLD MOZART
Frontispiece to the 1st ed. of his 'Violinschule', 1756
Engraving by Gottfried Eichler, Jr.

Reminiscences a quartet party at which, he remarks with pleasant under-statement, "the players were tolerable: not one of them excelled on the instrument he played, but there was a little science among them, which I dare say will be acknowledged when I name them:

THE FIRST VIOLIN	Haydn
THE SECOND VIOLIN	Baron Dittersdorf
THE VIOLONCELLO	Vanhall
THE TENOR	Mozart"

What a memorable evening that must have been! And there were surely many others like it when Prince Esterházy brought his household and

orchestra for a visit to Vienna. Mozart's father wrote to his daughter of a
similar occasion when his son's quartets were played, and Haydn said:
"Before God and as an honest man, I tell you that your son is the greatest
composer known to me either in person or by name. He has taste, and, what
is more, a most profound knowledge of composition."

Mozart composed only four more quartets after the "Haydn" set. One
in D major (K. 499) appeared by itself just after the production of *Figaro*,
and displays complete mastery of technique with smooth song-like melodies
in a style that he never quite recaptured. In 1789 he began a set of six
quartets for Frederick William II, King of Prussia, a good 'cellist, who
naturally expected an outstanding part for himself; so, in the three quartets
that he completed, Mozart wrote for the 'cello as elaborately as he could,
and made a virtue of necessity by his solution of the tricky problem in
balance caused by the prominence of the bass instrument. The 'cello receives
its full share of glory, but the other voices are skilfully regrouped where
compensating volume of tone is required. In two of these three quartets
the finales are marvels of contrapuntal lightness and grace, and are generally
more interesting than the first three movements which are rather sparsely
scored.

In all, Mozart produced only 26 quartets, as compared with Haydn's 84.
But he also wrote five string quintets (a type quite untried by Haydn,
excepting perhaps an early five-part *divertimento*) which are fully equal to
the quartets, and in some respects surpass them. The string quintet, including two violas, was really Mozart's own creation: a few had been composed before his time, but it was he who raised it to an art form. He preferred
the two violas and the warm, velvety texture that they imparted to the middle
voices, to the two 'cellos favoured by many other composers, including
Boccherini who wrote no fewer than 113 quintets in this form. The best-
known of Mozart's is the superb G minor, but the other three of his maturity
are equally fine, if less sombre and passionate. In all of them he uses the
extra instrument with consummate art and sympathy, both to weave new
patterns of tonal contrast and to develop still further the contrapuntal skill
of his "Prussian" Quartets. The last two quintets, in D and E flat, especially
in their headlong finales, contain good instances of the ambiguity of mood
and of the wry humour that pervade much of Mozart's late music, above all
his chamber works.

Besides quartets and quintets Mozart left three other equally important
works for strings—two duets for violin and viola, and a trio for violin,
viola and 'cello, the latter as arresting in its depth of feeling as in its technical

MICHEL DE LA BARRE WITH FRIENDS
La Barre is turning the page of his 'Sonates en Trio pour la flute traversière'
Painting ascribed to Robert Tournières, c. 1705

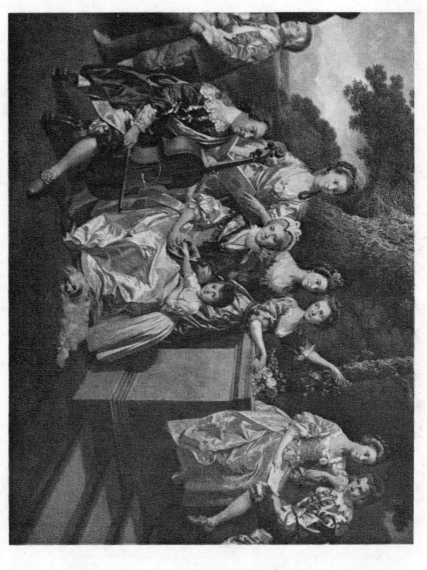

SIR WILLIAM AND LADY YOUNG WITH FOUR DAUGHTERS
Detail from the family portrait
Painting by Johann Zoffany, c. 1770

mastery over one of the most intractable of all chamber combinations. But all these string works represent only one side of Mozart's genius as a chamber composer: we should do him far less than justice if we failed to appreciate his astonishing achievement in other forms, many of which were of his own creating. These works which date from early youth to the last months of his life, fall into two broad classes, those with piano and those without.

Mozart was himself one of the great keyboard virtuosi of that day, so it was natural that his brilliant technique, which found its finest vehicle in the piano concertos, should be reflected in his chamber music for piano and strings. All of the seven piano trios are gay, melodious works, but only those in B flat and E major are outstanding. These two have something of the poetic tenderness of his great concertos. In all seven the piano dominates the action, and the violin and 'cello, though used more boldly than in Haydn's trios, especially as a contrasting tonal group, are still a long way from the freedom that Beethoven was to give them. On the other hand, in the masterly, richly coloured Trio for piano, clarinet and viola, all three parts are equally important, the central movement being a powerful minuet, one of the longest Mozart ever wrote. His two piano quartets are both of the same quality as this trio; they are practically miniature piano concertos. The balance between the keyboard and the three strings is almost ideal; for the latter are both treated as a block playing in close unison and harmony and paired off with clever spacing to combine or contrast with the piano. In quite half of the 42 violin sonatas the violin part can be omitted without much loss, but those in E minor, B flat (K. 454), E flat (K. 481) and A major (K. 526) are compositions of great vigour and unusual emotional range, in which Mozart entrusts to the violin an equal share in the expression of some of his most profound thoughts.

Virtuosity on the piano had little interest or attraction for Haydn, and this fact, combined with a certain lack of sympathy with wind instruments which he only remedied late in life, gives his chamber music (apart from the string quartet) an entirely different range and outlook from Mozart's, whose noble Quintet for piano, oboe, clarinet, horn and bassoon (1784) was a rare *tour de force*. Here Mozart revels in the best of both worlds, for he weds his command of piano technique to an affectionate understanding of wind instruments which had been his since boyhood. He himself said it was the finest work he had written up to that date, and what student of chamber music will dispute his judgment? This love of wind instruments and of experiments in timbre is manifest in a series of other works for one wind instrument and strings—four flute quartets, an oboe quartet, a horn quintet (with two violas) and the famous Clarinet Quintet—all gems of the finest water. Besides these, he composed a dry, sardonic little sonata for bassoon and 'cello, a quintet of ethereal beauty for flute, oboe, viola, 'cello and glass harmonica (his last chamber work) and some quintets, quartets, trios and duets for clarinets and basset-horns, the best of them unexpectedly solemn and profound.

A very popular field of music cultivated with success by both Haydn and Mozart (and by scores of other eighteenth-century musicians) is that of the divertimento and serenade. These count as chamber music by virtue of being performed with but a single player to each part, yet since they were written for festive and ceremonial occasions both indoors and out, they generally lack the intimacy characteristic of other chamber works of their era. The number of parts usually runs from six to ten, occasionally more. However, since this numerical increase set a fashion which continued in the nineteenth century—when in any case the scope of chamber music alters radically—we may as well conform to partly accepted usage, and enlarge our conception of the term to admit these delightful compositions. The names by which they were known—Cassation, Divertimento, Scherzando, Partita, Nocturne, Serenade—all amount to nearly the same thing, music for strings or wind, either alone or in combination, and in anything from four to six or seven movements.

Nearly all Haydn's works of this type were composed before 1775, and in many of them we can see him experimenting with the forms and blending of tone-colour which he was to elaborate and perfect in his symphonies, just as the baryton trios contained many of the seeds that matured in his quartets. His cassations, divertimenti and scherzandi are mainly scored for a string quartet (sometimes with the stiffening of a bass) plus one or two flutes, oboes (occasionally replaced by cors anglais) or horns. One set includes a good part for his Prince's baryton. Almost without exception, these works are gay and light as air. Soon after 1780 he composed a set of six Partitas, on a rather more massive scale, some for wind octet, some for two oboes, two horns, three bassoons and one serpent. Two are outstanding: one in G is bold and unusually vigorous and another in B flat has an extraordinarily fine set of variations as its last movement, in succession to a very beautiful slow movement entitled *Chorale St. Antoni*, on which Brahms wrote his immortal variations.

Just as Haydn produced these miscellaneous pieces either during his years of apprenticeship in Vienna, or for festive social occasions when he was employed first with Count Morzin and then with the Esterházys, so

Mozart's were composed principally for the court of the Archbishop of Salzburg, or for friends and patrons connected with it. After Mozart broke with the Archbishop and settled in Vienna (1781) he composed hardly any more serenades, but many slow movements of his greatest piano concertos have beautiful sections for wood-wind alone, reminiscent of his Salzburg technique. Mozart's earlier efforts cover roughly the same ground as Haydn's, but usually with bolder wind parts and a more song-like quality in the melodic line. Distinctly unusual are two divertimenti of 1773 for two flutes, five trumpets and four timpani. Five wind sextets (1776) for two oboes, two bassoons and two horns contain some of the most witty and entertaining music Mozart ever wrote, and the two wind octets of six years later rank among his very best works.

The summit of his wind music is reached in the *Gran Partita* of 1780 for thirteen instruments—two each of oboes, clarinets, bassoons, basset horns, four horns and a contrabassoon. It has seven movements, and is one of the outstanding instances of Mozart's use of a normally festive medium as a vehicle for some of his most personal and passionate utterances. Shortly before the completion of *Don Giovanni* in 1787 he wrote his "Musical Joke" for two horns and string quartet, which is a parody of inept chamber composers and, to a lesser extent, of clumsy players. Crude and pedestrian rhythms, monotonous climaxes, an undeveloped fugue, a violin cadenza that ends on something very near a whole-tone scale, and a final chord made up of five different keys—such are some of the ingredients of this most amusing piece. Soon afterwards came the delicious *Kleine Nachtmusik*, perhaps the best-known and most-played of all his chamber works.

SIX SONATAS FOR THE HARPSICHORD, OP. 2
Dedicated by Enrico Gavard des Pivets to Lady Carlisle
Engraved vignette, c. 1750

IV

A TRANSCENDENT GENIUS

HEN Beethoven began to compose chamber music, he could not but follow the style of Haydn and Mozart, and it was in this more intimate medium that he tried his wings before essaying the bolder flights of symphonies and concertos. From 1784 to 1792 Beethoven was a member of the court orchestra of the Elector at Bonn, who every day was "entertained by a small orchestra of two oboes, two clarinets, two horns and two bassoons". For this very combination Beethoven wrote two genial, if rather ponderous, pieces, a "Parthia" (i.e. partita) and a Rondino, both in E flat and dating from about 1792, from which year we also have a duo for two flutes, and three duos for clarinet and bassoon. When Beethoven left Bonn and settled in Vienna in 1792, he found there even ampler scope for his talents as a composer of wind music, both alone and with piano, which was beloved by all classes of society, and inspired by some of the finest players in Europe. A wind sextet (without the oboes) and a sextet for strings and two horns, both in E flat, and a trio in C for two oboes and cor anglais are outstanding among his chamber works of 1795-96, and in 1796 or 1797 he wrote a quintet for piano, oboe, clarinet, horn and bassoon (op. 16) in direct, but not always very successful imitation of Mozart's masterpiece for the same group.

On the other hand his Serenade in D (op. 25, 1797) for flute, violin and viola is incomparable—witty and exquisitely scored in gossamer texture. The Trio for clarinet, piano and 'cello (op. 11, 1797) is chiefly interesting for its clear proof that Beethoven had not at this time divined the soul of the clarinet as he had those of the flute and oboe; the work never really comes to life, but shows how tentative and uneven was his progress in his late twenties. The Sonata for horn and piano, however, inspired by the virtuosity of the great hornist Punto, is a very fine work, although composed in great haste. The culmination of Beethoven's wind ensembles is the Septet for clarinet, bassoon and horn, violin, viola, 'cello and bass, which was performed first at a private party given by Prince Schwarzenberg and soon after at a public concert on April 2, 1800. It is a straightforward, cheerful work, richly scored, but somewhat square and florid in style. It is simply good entertainment music which merited neither the lavish, uncritical praise bestowed on it nor Beethoven's own subsequent disparagement. The Septet was his last important chamber work including wind instruments,

LUDWIG VAN BEETHOVEN
Sketch for a lost portrait painted in 1818
Chalk drawing by August von Kloeber, c. 1817

apart from three short *Equali* for three trombones composed in 1812 for All Souls' Day at Linz. In these sombre and dignified pieces the interest lies in the effective spacing of chords rather than in melodic power: in an arrangement for voices all three were sung at Beethoven's funeral.

Surveying his wind chamber works as a whole, we feel that while he was the undoubted heir of the style and medium developed by Haydn and Mozart, he lacked the inspiration of environment which evoked from them such a wonderful variety of gay, light-hearted and unsophisticated music. Beethoven's conditions of life were freer and less artificial than theirs, yet his music in these forms lacks spontaneity just because the *raison d'être* of wind music was bound up with the social traditions of an age that was fast decaying and soon to be gone beyond recall. Happily it is quite otherwise with his chamber works for piano and strings and for strings alone: both groups were alive and flourishing, independent of past traditions. Furthermore, the piano was being developed to something of its modern sonority and power, so that it readily opened up new vistas of timbre and content. But quite early in his life he realised that for him there was a definite limit in the proportion of strings to keyboard. It is significant that after three piano quartets composed in 1785 he never again attempted to unite a powerful block of strings, potentially self-sufficient and of pure intonation, with the piano, which was tuned on a tempered scale. He found the trio for piano, violin and 'cello sufficiently sonorous for some of his grandest ideas, and in this form, as well as in sonatas for violin and piano and for 'cello and piano, his achievement is monumental.

Most of the small-scale works for violin and piano, such as the Variations on Mozart's "Se vuol ballare" (1792), the six German Dances (1795), and the Rondo in G (*c.* 1802) are tuneful and pleasant: the first important set is the three sonatas op. 12 (1797) which are real duos, with the violin given a prominence and freedom fully equal to that in Mozart's maturest sonatas. Beethoven infuses into op. 12 much of the freshness and lightness of the eighteenth century, combined with some bold strokes of modulation, and clever division of the melodic interest. The slow movement of the third sonata, that in E flat, is the first in all his chamber music to show real spiritual depth. In 1801 came the pair of sonatas op. 23 in A minor, and op. 24 in F major. In the latter Beethoven added to the traditional three movements a fourth in the form of a witty scherzo. Op. 23 is not wholly successful, but its Finale is interesting as foreshadowing the sombre energy of the "Kreutzer". Of the three sonatas comprising op. 30 only the third, in C minor, is outstanding: it is a little uneven, but the best of its four movements are worthy companions to the magnificent piano sonata in D minor, op. 31, no. 2, and have much in common, though on a smaller scale, with the dynamic power of the Fifth Symphony (1805-07). The famous "Kreutzer" Sonata in A major (op. 47, 1803) opens with a first movement of emotional power and technical brilliance almost unparalleled in chamber literature for the violin. But in its second movement—a set of graceful, but very difficult variations—and in the vigorous Finale, which is practically a tarantella in

A CONCERT PARTY AT THE HOUSE OF A FRENCH NOBLEMAN
By Gabriel Jacques de Saint-Aubin, 1724–80
Coloured engraving by A. J. Duclos

sonata form, Beethoven's inspiration flagged. The "Kreutzer" was composed at short notice for George Bridgetower, a mulatto violinist of British nationality, who visited Vienna in 1802; and to this haste may be attributed its unevenness. By far the finest and most difficult of all Beethoven's violin sonatas is the last, op. 96 in G, composed with great care in 1812 for Pierre Rode, a French player by whose pure style some of the work may have been inspired, for its four movements are a marvel of tranquil homogeneity. Its blend of delicate poise, latent strength and perfect balance of violin and keyboard has seldom been approached in sonatas by any later composer.

Beethoven's sonatas for 'cello and piano are the earliest of importance. With them, as with his violin sonatas, much discretion is needed on the part of the pianist in modern performance if he is to avoid swamping the 'cellist in the tremendous power of the twentieth-century grand piano. Against the lighter tone of the early-nineteenth-century instrument the 'cello stood out much more clearly and easily. Beethoven's op. 5 comprised two 'cello sonatas, no. 1 in F major and no. 2 in G minor, both written when he visited Berlin in 1796 for Duport, who was leading 'cellist at the court of King Frederick William II, himself an expert on this instrument. With an eye also to pleasing this monarch (just as Mozart had done in the

"Prussian" Quartets) Beethoven gave the 'cello a clear, independent part, covering all registers. Neither of these sonatas is wholly first-rate, but that in A major (op. 69, 1807) is a masterpiece, more attractive than those of op. 102 (no. 4 in G and no. 5 in D), bizarre and stormy works, full of the conflict of romantic crisis. Because of the superior sustaining power of the 'cello, it is far from easy to write a slow movement of adequate length without emphasising how short-lived are the notes of the piano, though this is less obvious in movements of quick or moderate tempo. In fact Beethoven burked the problem until the fifth and last sonata, where he solved it triumphantly. The difficulties of slow tempo are not so obtrusive in variation form, in which Beethoven wrote some admirable music for piano and 'cello. About 1796 he dedicated to Princess Lichnowsky a set of 12 variations on Handel's air "See the conquering Hero comes"; in 1797 he completed another set of twelve on Mozart's "Ein Mädchen oder Weibchen", from *Die Zauberflöte*, and in 1801 had recourse again to this favourite opera, choosing "Bei Männern welche Liebe fühlen" for a set of seven variations. The last two sets are full of most attractive and poetical ideas, and in fact rank high among Beethoven's lesser chamber works.

In his hands the scope of the violin and 'cello sonatas expanded to a breadth and intensity unimagined by Haydn and Mozart, but the piano trio underwent an even more portentous development. After a few negligible essays in this form, Beethoven composed three trios known as op. 1 which are of special interest for the deep impression they made on the devotees of chamber music in Vienna. He worked on them intermittently for nearly three years, and with them made his début as a composer at a concert given in Prince Lichnowsky's house. The finest is that in C minor, a work of amazing audacity and vehemence, wherein the strings are given their full rights in equal partnership with the piano. Of the two trios forming op. 70 (1808) the first in D is much the more interesting. It has a weird protracted Largo with a spasmodic melancholy theme played above long passages of tremolo that fluctuate from *pp* to *ff*. This movement has caused the work to be dubbed the "Ghost" Trio, and its underlying poetic ideas would appear, from Beethoven's sketch-books, to be the Witches' Scene in *Macbeth*. The E flat major Trio is lyrical and unclouded, planned on a very large scale. Three years later came the "Archduke" Trio in B flat (op. 97), so named from its dedication to the Archduke Rudolph. In this, one of Beethoven's noblest works, it is perhaps invidious to single out any one of the four movements, but the theme and variations forming the "andante cantabile" are truly sublime. Another fine trio (op. 121, 1823) consists of a solemn

DUET FOR VIOLIN AND VIOLA
From 'Trois Quatuors' by Giovanni M. Giornovichi, c. 1800
Engraved title-page from J. J. Hummel's edition

introductory Adagio with ten sprightly variations on a popular tune "Ich bin der Schneider Kakadu".

A solitary string duo for viola and 'cello, "with two *obbligato* eyeglasses", dating from 1796, is a whimsical piece, characteristic of his robust humour, and well written for an unrewarding combination. Beethoven's five string trios are all early works, but it is a great mistake to consider them as immature quartets. The equality of the violin, viola and 'cello is fully developed, and, although the level of the inspiration is uneven, there is no disputing his technical mastery of this intractable medium. Trio no. 1 in E flat (1793, revised 1797) and the Serenade in D (op. 8) are relatively unimportant, but of the three trios forming op. 9 (1797) those in G major and C minor are excellent. Yet he never recurred to this form; probably he felt it to be unsuited to his later ideas. For the combination of two violins, two violas and 'cello Beethoven wrote only two works, a Fugue in D (1817) and the Quintet in C (op. 29, 1801). The latter is distinguished by some unusually lovely melodies and by striking tremolo passages in the

SINGERS AND AUDIENCE
Silhouette sketches by Moritz von Schwind, 1838

powerful Finale, but as a whole the quintet is not of great importance in the growth of chamber music, since it does not represent much technical advance on Mozart's best work in this form.

Not until he was nearly thirty did Beethoven approach the string quartet, which had an older and more mature tradition than any other type of chamber music then extant. He meditated long before beginning his six quartets op. 18 but when they did appear in 1800 they marked a great advance on his other chamber works. The traces in op. 18 of the influence of Mozart and Haydn (whose pupil Beethoven was) are incontestable, but not so pronounced as we might expect. Later in life Beethoven said that without Haydn and Albrechtsberger, another of his masters, he could have made many blunders, and one thing his first quartets do avoid is overcrowding of ideas—a weakness that disfigures not a few of his early compositions. Probably the most potent influence was the quartets of his old master and valued friend Aloys Förster, in whose house musicians used to meet for chamber playing twice a week in 1794 and 1795. The immense pains that op. 18 cost Beethoven are well exemplified in the very opening phrase of no. 1 in F major. It looks simple enough, but the polishing and perfecting of it occupied sixteen pages of one of his sketch-books. Delightful and beautifully balanced though the six quartets are, they contain little to foreshadow the phenomenal strides that Beethoven's music was to make in the next few years. One outstanding passage is the mysterious episode entitled *La Malinconia* of no. 6 which breaks in ominously on the gay Finale.

MUSICIANS
Silhouette sketches by Moritz von Schwind, 1838

Much more daring passages are to be found in the 'Cello Sonata in G (op. 5, no. 2), in the C minor String Trio (op..9, no. 3), and scattered throughout the other chamber works in which Beethoven fostered his art before he matched it against the exacting demands of the quartet.

In 1806 he completed three quartets (no. 7 in F major, no. 8 in E minor, no. 9 in C major) which were published in 1808 as op. 59, with a dedication to Count Razumovsky, Russian Ambassador in Vienna. The fact that Beethoven wove Russian folk-tunes into the Finale of no. 7 and the Trio of no. 8 is of some interest, but it is much more important to realise that op. 59 as a whole marks the beginning of a new epoch in chamber music, just as momentous as that inaugurated in larger forms by the "Eroica" Symphony of 1804. Mere verbal description cannot do justice to the significant quality of these great quartets—still less to that of Beethoven's last five—and to single out any one movement for detailed mention would be invidious. It is more profitable to try to understand the reorientation of music that was taking place under the urge of the so-called Romantic Movement.

In much eighteenth-century music, emotion was incidental, and indeed artificial, being usually dictated by the need for melodic and formal contrast. But with the turn of the century, emotion becomes intensely subjective and craftsmanship, hitherto practised as part of the joy of creation, ceases to be an end in itself. Both are subservient to the expression of the composer's experience of life. And for Beethoven—lonely, ill, increasingly poor and

totally deaf—what more natural medium was there than the string quartet
to express and sublimate the suffering which seared his soul and body?
Not only was the quartet the most sincere and intimate form of music yet
evolved: it had for him the advantage of pure intonation which was audible
in his spiritual ear in a way that wind instruments and the piano from their
very nature could not hope to emulate.

The Razumovsky Quartets mark a new ideal in chamber music, not only
through their sustained and intensely personal feeling, but also because
they are conceived on a very large, almost symphonic scale. This naturally
demands great vehemence of expression. Quite early in his life Beethoven
wrote in one of his letters: "Power is the morality of men who stand out
from the rest, and it is also mine", and this sense of inner power, so early
evident in his String Trio op. 9, no. 3, Violin Sonata op. 30, no. 2 (both in
C minor), in the D minor Piano Sonata op. 31, no. 2, and in the G minor
'Cello Sonata, becomes more and more pronounced and aggressive as in
his loneliness he wrestled witʰ malign destiny, straining the bounds of the
chamber style to their utmost. Even his op. 18 quartets had aroused some
indignation: Bernhard Romberg, an eminent contemporary 'cellist, once
asked Spohr how he could play such "grotesque stuff"; Romberg is also
said to have thrown op. 59, no. 1 on the floor and stamped on it. Radicati,
a violinist who fingered op. 59 at Beethoven's request, relates: "I said to
him that surely he did not consider these works to be music? Beethoven
replied: 'Oh, they are not for you but for a later age!'" A contemporary
reviewer admitted their skill, but found them "generally incomprehensible".

By contrast with the "Razumovskys" the so-called "Harp" Quartet,
op. 74, a spirited and genial work, is retrograde. But the next, in F minor
(op. 95) marked *quartetto serioso*, is a noble composition; it is profoundly
moving and occupies much the same place in Beethoven's chamber music
as the String Trio in E flat does in Mozart's—it sums up the past and
clearly foretells future developments.

After completing his *Missa Solemnis* (1818-23) and his Choral Symphony
(1817-22) Beethoven realised that he had exhausted the possibilities of the
large choral and orchestral forms, just as the titanic op. 111 in C minor was
the Ultima Thule of the piano sonata. He had reached the material barriers
of musical architecture: the final profound development, unparalleled in
musical history, was to be found only in the metaphysical world of the
spirit, and for this the string quartet was the ideal medium. So in 1824, after
14 years' interval, Beethoven returned to chamber music, with three quartets
commissioned by Prince Galitzin (who wrote to the composer "Your genius

THEMES AND VARIATIONS ON SCOTTISH, WELSH AND IRISH AIRS
for pianoforte and flute or violin by Beethoven, op. 107
Autograph, 1818

is centuries in advance"), and went on to compose two more to satisfy himself. The first in E flat (op. 127) is a supremely happy work, and though on a large scale, is in the usual four movements. But for the next three (op. 132 in A minor, op. 130 in B flat major, and op. 131 in C sharp minor) this form was unsuitable, because their content radiates from a central experience. Thus op. 132 is in five movements, op. 130 in six, and op. 131 in seven; op. 131 was meant to be played without a break. Working on all three simultaneously, Beethoven gave them a shadowy unity through a fugal theme which he transformed to suit the spirit of each quartet.

In this stupendous trilogy, Beethoven explored wholly new regions of consciousness, in which he discovered new syntheses of spiritual experience. Each quartet co-ordinates an aspect of the same transcendent, mystical vision, which is expressed, as Wagner put it, in a serenity that passes beyond beauty. Chamber music here attains its apotheosis. The fifth quartet, op. 135 in F major, reverts to four separate movements, and moves on a less metaphysical plane. It is problematic in parts—as witness the Finale entitled *Der schwer gefasste Entschluss*, and the words written under its opening bars—but, except in the ineffable tranquillity of the slow movement, it is packed with boisterous, whimsical gaiety. Beethoven's last completed composition was a Finale for op. 130, written at the request of his friends to replace the *Grosse Fuge*, a movement of formidable complexity both to play and to understand, which originally rounded off the quartet. His chamber music ends on a note of unquestioning happiness.

V

TOWERING SHADOW AND NEW LIGHT

TO Franz Schubert (1797-1828), the most truly sociable of all the great musicians, the writing of chamber music was almost as natural a process as the writing of songs. Perhaps the most important factor in his upbringing was the love of music-making in his home, where the frequent playing of quartets went far to brighten the drabness of existence. Later in life, his social orbit included many groups of chamber players, both amateur and professional, whose demands were a constant source of inspiration. Schubert left 24 quartets, of which four early ones, written in 1811 and 1812, are lost, and two of 1813 consist of waltzes and minuets. Of the remaining 18 fully half were written before 1815 for performance in the family circle. He reached maturity as a quartet writer in 1814 with his op. 168 in B flat, and 1815 and 1816 brought two more lovely works, the G minor, and the E major (op. 125, no. 2). These are all unjustly neglected to-day, and the first of the quartets still regularly heard is a terse and tragic single movement in C minor of 1820. In 1824 Schubert wrote two masterly quartets, the A minor (op. 29) and the D minor, known, from the song whose melody he used for the theme of the final variations, as *Der Tod und das Mädchen*; his last quartet was the G major of 1826. These four works are of the highest genius, and their greatness lies in the reconciliation of classicism with romanticism. Spiritual unity compensates for a certain looseness of design.

These are the qualities which are intensified in his greatest chamber work, the String Quintet in C major of 1828. In this majestic, sonorous composition, which sets a worthy coping-stone on the edifice of classical chamber music, Schubert followed Boccherini by using two 'cellos in preference to two violas. The whole quintet is as moving a personal document as any of Beethoven's last quartets: the Adagio, with its mood of black, resigned despair, is one of the most terrifying things in all chamber music. No less remarkable is the conquest of this mood in a glorious Finale, in which Schubert's indomitable spirit soars on wings as strong as those of the superb C major Symphony of this same year.

His remaining chamber works run to nearly a score, varying greatly in form, but very uneven in quality and importance. Only four which have stood the test of time have found a regular place in the chamber repertoire. There are two exuberant piano trios, op. 99 and 100, both dating from

SCHUBERT PLAYING AT A SOIRÉE OF BARON SPAUN
Drawn after Schubert's death
By Moritz von Schwind, 1868

1827, and the famous "Trout" Quintet, scored for piano, violin, viola, 'cello and double-bass, and designed, rather unusually, in five movements, the fourth being a charming set of variations on the song "The Trout". In the glorious Octet of 1824, comprising string quartet, double-bass, clarinet, bassoon and horn, Schubert was paying tribute to Beethoven's "Septet", while he actually wrote the work for Count von Troyer, who was himself a clarinettist and chamber enthusiast, and also chief officer of the household to Archduke Rudolph, Beethoven's patron. Among Schubert's lesser chamber pieces, one of the most engaging and original is a set of variations for flute and piano, on the song "Trockne Blumen" from "Die schöne Müllerin".

In chamber music Schubert found a natural utterance wherein he freed himself from the towering shadow of Beethoven much more easily and completely than ever he did in his numerous piano sonatas. Yet it is difficult to detect any consistent and progressive development towards complete mastery of the many chamber forms that he essayed. He left a copious store of delectable and charming music, but apart from a handful of works of superlative quality, it is generally lacking in the ballast of seriousness which makes for a safe voyage among the treacherous shoals of chamber composition. We feel that Schubert rather sought in it a means to the expression of some relief from the harrowing troubles and disappointments of his life which not even his buoyant spirit could always surmount. He often tried to bolster up a certain flabbiness of design by fanciful digressions which sometimes took on a hectic tinge from what amounted to an abuse of his genius for colourful modulation. None but the blindest admirer of his chamber music can boggle at these facts, which we must see in true perspective because, although it is indisputably in the true classical tradition, its greatness coexists with the elements of decline.

So engrossing is the part played by Haydn, Mozart, Beethoven and Schubert in bringing classical chamber music to perfection that we are apt to forget that they did not work in splendid isolation, and to overlook a host of lesser composers whose chamber pieces must have run to several thousand between 1750 and 1830. Space permits the mention of but a few, typical of the scores of fine craftsmen whose polished and witty music contributed much to the graciousness and gaiety of social life all over Europe. Here are five, the best of whose music deserves a permanent place in the chamber music repertoire: J. C. Bach (1735-82), who spent most of his life in London; Boccherini (1743-1805), who divided his time between the courts of Prussia and Spain; Gossec (1734-1829), the "Grand Old Man" of French music, who carried the classical tradition beyond the Revolution; Hummel (1778-1837), a pupil of Mozart; and Weber (1786-1826), brilliant in his few chamber works as in all others. All these furthered this branch of music by experimenting with fresh instrumental groups, or by developing traditional forms on new lines.

The essence of musical romanticism was incompatible with the blend of conciseness, unity and balance which was the basis of the classical ideal in chamber music, and after 1830 the seeds of decay germinated very quickly. Orchestral treatment of the string quartet, which we noticed in Beethoven's op. 59, increases in frequency, and the clear-cut outline of the classical groupings and proportions becomes blurred. At the same time, however, we must readily admit that chamber music, because of its smaller range and limited colour, did not suffer from the excesses which swelled the larger instrumental forms to such grandiose dimensions during the nineteenth century.

The unchanged physical nature of the quartet made it unsuitable for programme music on a large scale, but the few works of this kind that were attempted are unusually interesting. In chamber groups with a piano, the ever-growing power of the concert-grand evoked a new style with a volume

A VENETIAN CHAMBER REHEARSAL
of an Italian Opera
Painting ascribed to Marco Ricci, c. 1710

THE BUSCH QUARTET
Painting by Joseph Läuscher, 1937

of sound requiring a small hall rather than a large room. And although chamber playing continued to flourish in private circles, it also entered the field of commercial enterprise. (One of the first quartets to travel widely was that of the brothers Müller, who in 1831 began to tour Europe with a repertory consisting of the quartets of Haydn, Mozart and Beethoven.) After Beethoven, as after Bach, real progress was only possible by re-orientation; therefore we must assess all these changes at their real value, and refrain from applying a classical yardstick to the new ideals of romantic chamber music. Since these ideals owed much of their vitality to the skill with which composers adapted the more malleable elements of the classical tradition, we can find a continuous pattern of beauty strong enough to offset certain aberrations and weaknesses.

Mendelssohn and Schumann, who helped to inaugurate the romantic movement, were both exceptionally fine pianists and also enthusiastic chamber players; but only the latter used the piano progressively as a chamber instrument. Mendelssohn's best piece is his String Octet, composed when he was 16, a product of something like real genius. But in his quintets, quartets and piano trios, he too often attempted the Beethovenian grand manner, which usually brought him to grief except in the fine D minor Trio. Schumann's best work, on the other hand, bears the impress of his brilliant technique, especially in his Piano Quintet, Quartet, and the Trio in D minor. These are only marred by his habit of doubling the string parts on the keyboard. There is no doubt that the diffuseness of his later chamber music is largely due to the mental trouble that weakened his powers of concentration. His *Märchenerzählungen* for clarinet, viola and piano is a colourful and charming essay in lighter vein, corresponding to Mendelssohn's pieces for piano, clarinet and basset-horn.

Brahms's profound knowledge of musical history never allowed him to forget that he was heir to the great classical tradition, and Beethoven's shadow hung more heavily over him than ever it did over Mendelssohn or Schumann. Indeed, the greater part of Brahms's creative life revolved round his efforts to reconcile the romantic streak in his nature with the austere demands of classical formalism. In chamber music as in all else his development was carefully planned, beginning with the massive Piano Trio op. 8 (originally composed in 1856 and remodelled in 1891) against which the more restrained String Sextet in B flat seems a reaction. The two piano quartets well represent Brahms's early compromise between the classic and the romantic, further developed in the grand Piano Quintet in F minor, op. 34. After another sextet, in G (op. 36), he graduated to string quartets, but having composed three he realised that this form was too restricted for his ideas. While the A minor Quartet (op. 51, no. 2) is patently orchestral in texture and sonority, in the two superb string quintets (op. 88 and 111) the extra viola gives a greater reserve of power. Another piano quartet, in C minor (op. 60), proves further that the combination of keyboard and strings was a most congenial medium. The Trio for piano, horn and violin (op. 40) is a masterpiece for a hitherto unused combination. In his three violin sonatas, all late works, Brahms made the first real advance in this form since Beethoven's op. 96 in G. But occasionally the piano part is overloaded to an extent that makes it hard for the violin to be heard as an equal partner, and so spoils the effect of these majestic works. With the mellowing years, Brahms's chamber style became more refined, and allowed him to strike a well-nigh perfect balance in his noble Clarinet Quintet (op. 115), and in the Trio for clarinet, 'cello and piano (op. 114) which has been overshadowed by the Quintet. His two sonatas for clarinet or viola and piano (op. 120) are works of rare beauty, inspired, like the Clarinet Quintet and Trio, by Mühlfeld, the foremost clarinettist of that day. With Brahms must be mentioned his close friend Joachim (1831-1907), the Hungarian violinist, whose playing influenced Brahms's writing for the violin, and whose famous string quartet set a European standard in chamber music for nearly forty years.

MARIA AND TERESA MILANOLLO
Two famous girl performers, about 1840
Lithograph from Charles Wanner's 'Souvenir'

VI

'INFINITE IS THE SWEETE VARIETIE'

HEN the flood of national feeling spread all over Europe after
W 1815, it affected chamber music far less than the larger forms, even
in Russia where native composers were at last coming into their own.
Tchaikovsky (1840-93) was the first to write chamber music that has lived,
comprising three quartets composed before 1875, a piano trio (1882) and a
string sextet entitled *Souvenir de Florence* (1890). He did not use many actual
folk-melodies—the most famous is in the Andante of the first quartet—but
many of his themes, especially those of a characteristically elegiac mood,
have an unmistakably Russian flavour. Borodin (1834-87)—aptly described
as "the supreme justification of the amateur in music"—composed two
quartets, in 1878 and 1880 respectively. These brilliant works were born of
his own devotion to chamber playing: the Nocturne of no. 2 has become
world-famous. On the other hand S. I. Taneiev (1856-1915), a pupil of
Tchaikovsky, was a learned theoretician, who left a number of important
pieces—six quartets, two quintets and trios—in the classical tradition.
The only composer really comparable with Taneiev in all Russian chamber
music is Glazunov (1865-1936), one of the group of St. Petersburg nationalists. His first two quartets have a strong Slavonic tinge, which is even
more marked in his *Novelettes*, delightful little genre pictures notable for
their complete break with the tradition of sonata form. Likewise, a Suite for
string quartet ends with a lilting waltz. His third quartet, the "Slavonic",
contains a mazurka in place of a scherzo, and concludes with a picture of a
Slavonic festival, but in his String Quintet and fourth and fifth quartets,
he returned to classical orthodoxy of form and content.

One of the most influential figures in Russian chamber music was
M. P. Belaiev, a wealthy amateur, who in 1885 set up as a publisher and
concert-promoter for the benefit of his compatriots, and later made his
house a musical centre on Friday evenings. In his honour several longish
works were compositely written by various musicians, notably a quartet
in four movements linked by a theme on the musical notes of his name—
Be (= B flat), La (= A) and F. The first movement was by Rimsky-Korsakov
(1844-1908), the second, a Scherzo, by Liadov (1855-1914), followed by a
Spanish Serenade by Borodin and a Finale by Glazunov. Two other sets
of these delightful pieces, published under the title *Les Vendredis*, are a
monument to one of the most fruitful periods in the history of chamber

music. Belaiev's influence was felt indirectly after his death in 1904, through the numerous pupils of the musicians in his circle of friends. Arensky (1861-1906), for instance, was a pupil of Rimsky-Korsakov, and wrote a fine piano trio in D minor, a piano quintet and two quartets, the second of which (for violin, viola and two 'cellos) includes variations on a theme of Tchaikovsky's.

In the Czech national group of composers, those who excelled in chamber music were Smetana, Dvořák, Fibich and Suk. Smetana (1824-84) left a piano trio and two string quartets, entitled *From my Life*, which are most interesting as they attempt to portray incidents from his own life. Fibich (1850-1900) wrote a quartet, Theme and Variations for string quintet, an unusual quintet for piano, clarinet, horn, violin and 'cello, and a piano trio and quartet. All these are works of great vigour, rich colouring and striking rhythms including, in the Piano Quartet, the polka, the national dance, here first used in chamber music.

In modern performance these two nationalists are far outstripped by the popularity of Dvořák (1841-1904) who has a unique place in the history of chamber music. His chief works are a string trio, eight string quartets, a string quintet and sextet, a piano quintet, two piano quartets, and three piano trios. In all these his idiom is unmistakable: both rhythm and melody are highly original, sometimes closely akin to Slavonic folk music. In the Quartet in F (the "Nigger") and the Quintet in E flat Dvořák blended most effectively some negro rhythms, which attracted him during a visit to America, with his own nostalgic lyricism.

In nearly every other country chamber music has been written with a national flavour, as by Grieg and Svendsen in Norway, by Casella, Malipiero and Pizzetti in Italy, and by Turina in Spain. Dohnányi (b.1877) and Kodály (b.1882) have both written attractive chamber compositions; but by far the greatest of the Hungarians is Bartók (1881-1945), whose unique sense of tonal values partly derives from folk-music. His six quartets, ranging from 1908 to 1939, are profound and compelling works, for in originality of style and construction and in novel treatment of stringed instruments they stand alone. Who shall say that Bartók is not the Beethoven of the twentieth century?

French chamber music had never been subject to strong foreign influences, so that when its late renaissance began, after the political disasters of 1870, it was free from nationalistic tendencies. Under Louis Philippe the "Cercle de Bèze" in Paris had assiduously fostered chamber playing, but the first creative impetus came chiefly from César Franck (1822-90), whose

JOSEPH JOACHIM ACCOMPANIED BY CLARA SCHUMANN
Drawing by Adolph Menzel, 1854
Print Room, Berlin

influence has lasted long after the more brilliant chamber works of his contemporaries Lalo and Saint-Saëns have largely been forgotten. (The latter's Septet for piano, trumpet, string quartet and double-bass well merits occasional performance.) Franck's chamber music is notable more perhaps for construction than for content. Though packed with glowing colour and rich harmonic resources, many of the movements are very long. (The magnificent violin sonata, composed for Ysaye, is an exception.) But Franck did make one important technical advance by introducing the unity of so-called "cyclic form", the elaborate use of one principal tune for transformation in successive movements.

Foremost among Franck's pupils who carried on his tradition and ideals were d'Indy (1851-1931), Chausson (1855-99) and Lekeu (1870-94). D'Indy was particularly ardent in his use of cyclic form, as in the noble String Quartet in E major. But he was really too learned a composer to succeed completely in the chamber style, although the great eloquence of his best pieces makes them worthy of performance. One of his pupils was Roussel (1869-1937), a composer of impeccable taste, whose Serenade for harp, flute and string trio is truly exquisite chamber music. A greater master was Fauré (1845-1924), who left ten chamber compositions, representing a different tradition from Franck's teaching. More orthodox in construction, they reached a degree of refinement in style that became cool and delicate to the point of evanescence.

It was left to Debussy (1862-1918), the leader of French musical impressionism, to strike out on entirely new lines. His solitary Quartet, first performed in 1894, created a sensation. It combined freedom of rhythm with a startling fluidity of line, form and harmony, deriving in part from Borodin, whose quartets Debussy had heard at the concerts of Russian music organised by Belaiev during the Paris Exhibition of 1889. In Debussy's Quartet and to a lesser extent in his Sonatas for 'cello and violin, and in his Trio for flute, harp and viola, French chamber music finds its perfect counterpart to the paintings of Monet, who laid emphasis on the shifting play of light rather than on actual objects.

The second great impressionist was Ravel (1875-1937), who concentrated rather less on "atmospheric" effect, and recaptured something of the clarity and precision of the eighteenth century. His chamber masterpiece is the Introduction and Allegro for string quartet, flute, clarinet and harp (1906). Indeed, poetical use of the rippling tone-colour of the harp, as in this lovely work, is quite characteristic of much of modern French chamber music. We meet it again in the Andante and Scherzo for chromatic harp and string quartet by Florent Schmitt (b.1870).

With the turn of the century, the inevitable reaction set in against the eloquence of Franck, the scholasticism of d'Indy and the impressionism of Debussy. It culminated in the activities of the group of composers known as "Les Six"—Poulenc, Auric, Honegger, Durey, Tailleferre and Milhaud —and especially in their numerous chamber pieces, issued roughly between 1910 and 1925. With Erik Satie (the whimsical composer of piano works with such titles as "Pièces en forme de poire", "Choses vues à droite et a gauche") for their prophet, and Jean Cocteau for their literary spokesman, they made a special cult of jazz and the style of the music-halls. The resultant music was often of deliberate banality, coupled with extreme ingenuity. Milhaud, for example, in his quartets has written many passages in two or

VIOLIN RECITAL IN HONOUR OF TWO INDIAN PRINCES
The violinist is probably Wilma Norman-Neruda (later Lady Hailé)
Painting by James Tissot, c. 1876

more keys simultaneously. But such tendencies have not been confined to France alone among European countries.

In Germany and Austria especially, since about 1900, the trend of chamber composition has faithfully reflected the crisis visible in the larger musical forms. Here only a very brief summary of it can be attempted. Schönberg, Berg and Webern, rebelling against the romanticism of Wagner, produced many pieces for new and ingenious combinations that sometimes included a vocal part. They developed the so-called "atonal" style which dispenses with traditional key relationships and relies on a system of twelve notes of equal value, Schönberg's *Pierrot Lunaire* (1912), scored for piano, flute, clarinet, violin and 'cello, with a reciter, and Berg's *Lyric Suite* (1927) for string quartet were landmarks in their day.

Hindemith and Křenek, both fluent composers of quartets, have been the chief exponents of "workaday music" (*Gebrauchsmusik*), in which the revolt against the doctrine of "art for art's sake" was pressed to its utmost. In the 1920's both these musicians were attempting to write chamber pieces in a "neo-classical" style, by reviving some of the stricter forms of the eighteenth century, and clothing them in modern harmonies. The use of intervals as small as a sixth and a twelfth of a tone—known as microtones—was introduced into chamber music principally by Alois Hába (b.1893), a Czech composer, who wrote a dozen pieces in this highly original harmonic idiom. He has had a number of followers, but such music is too subtle ever to attract a very large public.

These and many other innovations and experiments have contributed sadly little to the true progress of chamber music, which can never flourish and put forth new branches when nourished on arid theory, trivial ideas and emotional expression so superficial as often to seem non-existent. In works of this nature, the communication of sincere, intimate feeling is almost impossible, if only because the number of hearers who can genuinely appreciate Webern's String Trio (1927), for example, is very small indeed. Further, the technical demands of atonal and microtonal chamber music are severe, being, in fact, beyond the range of all save professional musicians or highly skilled amateurs. (But it should be admitted that the general standard of chamber playing seems to have risen in recent years, and this must be partly due to the acceptance of the challenge offered by difficult modern works.) This whole phase, however, was on the wane by the 1930's and there are now some signs of new and healthier life. In France, for example, Poulenc and Honegger, having abandoned the jejune smartness of "Les Six", have enriched the chamber repertoire with pieces of truly Gallic wit and delicacy.

During all this era of flux and uncertainty there have been a number of great musicians who stood aside from contemporary fashions and experiments. Some of them, though primarily interested in the larger forms, have been unable to resist the challenge implicit in the discipline and limitations of the chamber style, and so have produced one or two characteristic and highly original pieces, with all the charm of miniatures. How many people who delight in Gounod's *Faust* and other operas are aware that in 1885 he composed a delightful Nonet for wind instruments, which reveals quite a different side of his genius? Another little-known work for wind is Richard Strauss's sonorous Serenade for thirteen instruments, inspired by Mozart's masterpiece for a similar group. This is early Strauss (1882), in a very different vein from his tone-poems and operas.

Sibelius's solitary and deeply personal quartet entitled *Voces Intimae* (1908) is important because it reproduces on a small scale the mature style of his great symphonies. He states his melodies not as complete entities to be

JOSEPH JOACHIM AND HIS QUARTET
Painting by Lajos Bruck, c. 1880

built up in the orthodox way, but presents them in the form of fragments which are assembled as each movement grows into shape. No other chamber composer has attempted this difficult though fascinating technique. Similarly, Bruckner's two broad and melodious pieces for string quintet transfer to a smaller medium much of the spiritual depth of his masses and symphonies. Let Verdi be cited as another example of specialised genius departing from its normal vein. The String Quartet (1873), his sole instrumental work, contains the essence of all that is happiest in his operas: its style is unpretentious, and it bubbles over with gay tunes and rhythms perfectly moulded to the unwonted medium. Finally, among these stepchildren of the great orchestral and symphonic composers, we cannot pass over the Chamber Concerto for harpsichord, clarinet, flute, oboe, violin and 'cello (1927) by Manuel de Falla. Here he gives us much of the piquant vigour of his famous *Nights in the Gardens of Spain*, blending dance rhythms with a deliberately archaistic refinement of manner. This miniature concerto is one of the most attractive of all his works.

In America, chamber music as a branch of composition was late in taking root, and did not really establish itself until the 1870's. By then G. W. Chadwick (1854-1931) was coming to the fore in a group of composers who had studied under German masters in Europe. Another potent influence was that of Dvořák from 1892 to 1895 when he held the directorship of the National Conservatorium of Music in New York. Much chamber music has since been composed for a great variety of new instrumental groups, partly under the healthy stimulus that comes from the many benefactions of Mrs. Elizabeth Sprague Coolidge. From 1917 to 1924 she organised the elaborate Berkshire festivals, and from 1925 onwards chamber competitions and concerts have been held through her munificence in the Library of Congress at Washington, in a specially built auditorium. These events have attracted composers and performers from all over the world, not least the talent of European refugees, to whom, much to their own enrichment, the United States have ever been hospitable.

But up to now no American-born composer has arisen as a master of chamber music in the great tradition. Of a number of notable musicians who have become naturalised Americans, C. M. Loeffler (1861-1935), of Alsatian origin, and a pupil of Joachim, produced a few chamber works of outstanding quality. One of far greater stature, however, is Ernest Bloch, born at Geneva in 1880. He has written two string quartets, a piano quintet, a suite for viola and piano, and two violin sonatas, all these bearing the impress of a powerful and outstandingly original mind. They are characterised by some movements of impassioned gloom, and by passages combining extraordinary brilliance with frenetic energy. The future, in the hands of the younger generation as represented by such gifted composers as Samuel Barber, is distinctly promising.

After the revival of chamber music had begun in England in the 1880's it pursued a fresh and fruitful path. It has been virtually unaffected by Continental trends, and has drawn continually on the rich melodic store of folk-music. The first task of this great renaissance was obviously to throw off the long tyranny of alien influences, and then in the interest of native talent to overcome the public prejudice and apathy rooted in the conviction that only German composers could write good quartets. The leaders were Parry (1848-1918), Stanford (1852-1924) and McEwen (b.1868). The extent of the obstacles they had to overcome may be gauged from the fact that when McEwen's fourth quartet appeared in 1903, it was the first for over a century by a British composer to be printed in England. Even as undergraduates, Parry at Oxford and Stanford at Cambridge had done much to

HAYDN IN D MAJOR
Arnold Rosé and his Quartet playing in London
Painting by Ethel Macmillan, 1943

promote a notable revival of amateur chamber playing. They continued their enthusiastic labours later at the Royal Academy and the Royal College of Music.

In time these and many other activities, in schools, colleges and private clubs all over the country, went to swell an ever-growing wave of chamber playing, and apparently this life-giving tide has yet to reach the flood. Many series of concerts have flourished for long periods. Three of the most notable that have fostered public interest in London were the "Pops", given once and, later, twice weekly at St. James's Hall from 1858 to 1898; the South Place Sunday concerts which lasted from 1887 to 1940 and, after an interruption due to the war, were resumed in 1945; and the National Gallery Concerts which drew large audiences daily from 1940 to 1946, and seemed to thrive on the dangers and difficulties of war-time. Another institution of great value is the summer school of chamber music held at Downe House in Hampshire, where players of all grades meet informally for practice, and are coached in their art by experts under the genial leadership of Ivor James.

In the last sixty years practically every British composer of repute has contributed to the enlargement of the chamber repertoire. Some came to this type of music late in life, as did Elgar (1857–1934), whose String Quartet, Piano Quintet and Violin Sonata are mellow and highly individual masterpieces. To others, it has been a life-long and natural form of expression. Others again were particularly stimulated by the "Phantasy" prize compositions instituted in 1905 by W. W. Cobbett, a generous and enthusiastic amateur, who held much the same place in the chamber music life of England as Belaiev did in that of Russia. Cobbett's aim was to revive the tradition of the seventeenth-century fancy. He stipulated that all pieces submitted should be short, in one movement only, and for strings alone, ranging from duets to quintets. This idea evoked many lovely "Phantasies" including fine works by Vaughan Williams, Bridge and Ireland, who have all written other excellent chamber music.

Another source of potent inspiration has been the masterly viola-playing of Lionel Tertis, who persuaded such gifted chamber composers as Bax, Dale and York Bowen to write pieces specially for this expressive, long-neglected instrument. A particular excellence of British composers has been the introduction of a vocal part into a chamber work, something after the manner of Scarlatti's chamber cantatas of the early eighteenth century. Such compositions as Vaughan Williams's song cycle on Housman poems, "Wenlock Edge" (tenor and piano quintet), van Dieren's "Sonetto VII of Spenser's *Amoretti*" (baritone and mixed wind and string octet), and Warlock's setting of four of Yeats's poems, "The Curlew" (tenor, strings, flute and cor anglais), are beautiful, original and deeply expressive. They open up a new vista of great possibilities.

Taking a general view of British chamber music during the last fifty years, we can reflect with some pride that though we have not produced works equal in significance to the quartets of a Haydn or a Beethoven, the level of genuine creativeness has undoubtedly remained high. Do not the quartets of Walton, Britten and Tippett ensure that this level will be maintained, if not surpassed? The successful pursuit of variety has not weakened a tradition that was sound and vigorous, even though it had lain dormant for over a century. The works of a host of composers besides those mentioned here form, it is true, only one of the many tributaries flowing into

AT A NATIONAL GALLERY CONCERT
Max Rostal, the violinist, November 1945
Sketch by Stella Schmolle

the main stream of chamber music, but its surface is brighter than that of many broader European currents.

We have seen how, during the nineteenth century, chamber music, which had stood for the communication of the composer's intimate thoughts in intimate surroundings, extended its scope to the concert hall. Yet the physical limitations of true chamber combinations should preclude performance in very large halls, and so help to preserve this music from the worst effects of publicity and commercialism. Although it will never be music for the many, it is perhaps unfortunate that the effort of concentration needed for real appreciation has fostered the delusion that it is a highly intellectual pleasure for the few. True, in most chamber works the first movement, though but one of four, is usually in sonata form; yet this form is also the unquestioned basis of all the popular classical symphonies and overtures. However, there are hopeful signs to-day of an increase in the numbers of those who make leisure, as hearers or performers, to pursue the pleasures of chamber music. Besides being "the music of friends" it is, and always has been, the art of the musical idealist. In this, perhaps, lies the secret of its enduring quality, and of its true spirit, never more finely expressed than by Henry Peacham in his book *The Compleat Gentleman*, written in 1622, when all secular music was fundamentally chamber music:

> *Infinite is the sweete varietie that the Theorique of*
> *Musicke exerciseth the mind withal, as the contemplation*
> *of proportions, of Concords and Discords, diversitie of*
> *Moods and Tones, infiniteness of Invention, &c. But I*
> *dare affirme, there is no one Science in the world, that so*
> *affecteth the free and generous spirit, with a more delight-*
> *full and in-offensive recreation, or better disposeth the minde*
> *to what is commendable and vertuous.*

INDEX

(The figures in italics refer to the pages on which illustrations appear)

BIBLIOGRAPHY

Bruno AULICH and Ernst HEIMERAN : *The Well-Tempered String Quartet*. Novello, 1938.

Walter W. COBBETT : *Cobbett's Cyclopedic Survey of Chamber Music*. 2 vol. O.U.P., 1929-30.

Thomas F. DUNHILL : *Chamber Music: a treatise for students*. Macmillan, 1913.

John D. HAYWARD : *Chamber Music for Amateurs*. 'Strad' Office, 1923.

Charles W. HUGHES : *Chamber Music in American Schools*. The Author : New York, 1933.

Nicholas KILBURN : *Chamber Music and its Masters in the Past and in the Present*. New ed. by G. E. H. Abraham. Reeves, 1932.

Ernst H. MEYER : *English Chamber Music . . . from the Middle Ages to Purcell*. Lawrence & Wishart, 1946.

M. D. Herter NORTON : *String Quartet Playing*. Carl Fischer : New York, 1925.

George STRATTON and Alan FRANK : *The Playing of Chamber Music*. O.U.P., 1935.

Sir Donald F. TOVEY : *Essays in Musical Analysis: Chamber Music*. O.U.P., 1944.

Richard WALTHEW : *The Development of Chamber Music*. Boosey, 1909.